Guitar World Presents

The Bonehead's Guide to Effects

**Published by Hal Leonard Corporati~
in cooperation with Harris Public~
and Guitar World Ma**
**Guitar World is a registere~
of Harris Publication~**

HAL•LEONARD®
CORPORATION

7777 W. BLUEMOUND RD. P.O. BOX 13819 MILWAUKEE, WI 53213

Guitar World Presents

The Bonehead's
Guide to Effects

by Dominic Hilton

ISBN #0-7935-9801-X

Visit Hal Leonard Online at
www.halleonard.com

◆ Executive Producer
Brad Tolinski

◆ Producer
Carol Flannery

◆ Book Packager, Designer
Ed Uribe for Dancing Planet MediaWorks™

◆ Cover and Inside Illustrations
Jim Ryan

Foreword

One of my favorite effects-related memories started with your average family outing. Being forced out of my bedroom, with its stereo and beloved electric guitar, into the gray light of a Sunday afternoon put me in a typical teenage mood. Much countryside and rain-soaked sightseeing concluded with a reluctant visit to a wayside antique/junk store. While my folks dug out some bargains, I miserably picked through the dusty shelves until I came upon something decidedly stompboxlike. The store owner let me have it for peanuts, thinking it was a broken transistor radio. The small wedge-shaped case was made of orange Tolex-covered wood with a metal plate covered with "chickenhead" knobs. Unfortunately, the cover plate was so scuffed that none of the original markings were readable, not even a name or logo as a clue. Inside, a few stray wires told me it was going to need a visit to my friend the electronic engineer. He cleaned it, fixed the loose contacts, and put in a fresh battery. It was now technically safe and working, but neither of us knew what it actually did.

I hooked it up between my guitar and amp, then started messing with the controls. The deep-sea rumbles, fuzzy screams, stratospheric blips and aquatic gurgles that leapt out took us both by surprise. I couldn't tell if it was even working properly, but it sounded fantastic, and like nothing else I'd heard. Whatever it was had probably come from early-'70s Japan in the experimental heyday of stompbox effects. Maybe it was an octaving-fuzz-auto-wah, or something entirely different. I just called it Thing. Years later, in a moment of stupidity, I traded Thing in for a guitar case, and have regretted it ever since. Thing summed up all the best things about effects: being inspiring, unexpected and eccentric. The lesson? Hold on to your effects even when you think you're bored of them. If you they inspired you once, they'll inspire you again.

~DH

P.S. If Thing is reading this, please call.

The author would like to thank Brad Tolinski and Paul Riario at Guitar World magazine, Jim Ryan for his superb cartoons, Ed Uribe at Dancing Planet MediaWorks, Neville Marten and Sarah Clark at Guitarist magazine, Bean and all those fun-filled-effects manufacturers for the photos.

About the Author:

DOMINIC HILTON is a freelance writer and incurable gearhead who enjoys spreading the word for Guitar World, Guitar World Acoustic, Guitarist, Bassist and Total Guitar magazines. He also enjoys breeding Energizer Bunnies to supply his stompbox battery needs.

Table of Contents

Introduction

So what is a guitar effect? Well, it's literally anything that has an effect on the sound of your guitar. Even back in the 1950s, when the electric guitar was but an infant, guitarists started to develop ways to alter their sound. The simple controls of the guitar were used to produce violinlike swells and subtle vowel sounds. Later, weird mechanical contraptions with motors, loops of tape and revolving drums were commandeered in the pursuit of strange new noises. By the early '70s the "silicon revolution" made it possible for effects manufacturers to squeeze exciting sounds into small, portable cases, and the stompbox was born. The race for fuzzier, groovier and funkier effects was on, and guitarists couldn't get enough of them. With the advent of the computer age, digital technology and even computer software has been used as yet another way to bend our tone out of shape. In fact, there is very little that hasn't been used one way or another to produce guitar effects.

So why use them? Simply because they are inspiring to play and exciting to listen to. Some players, like Jimi Hendrix, developed a large part of their style around certain effects; others use them as a chef would use spices—a pinch here and there to add some zing. Many classic songs wouldn't be the same, or even have been written, without effects; imagine the Stones' "Satisfaction" without the waspy guitar riff, or Led Zeppelin's "Dazed And Confused" without the eerie psychedelic atmosphere. This book is intended as a guide through these sonic illusions, to help you understand how they work and what they sound like. Be warned though, it's easy to become a stompbox junkie... just one more fuzz box, then I'll quit, honest.

Construction

Effects manifest themselves in many forms, from tiny circuits built into the guitar itself to huge rack systems that look like part of the NASA space program. Whichever format is used, all of these devices rely on an electronic circuit to alter the sound on its way from the **guitar** to the **amplifier**. Essentially, the guitarist plays and causes the strings to vibrate; this sound is captured by the guitar's **pickup** and travels down a cable to the amplifier, where it gets shaped and made louder. An effect will come between the guitar and amplifier and, when it is switched on, will take that signal and modify it before it is amplified. In its simplest form this will be a single effect, usually in the form of an **effects pedal**, or **stompbox**, connected by two leads. The following simple diagram shows the path of the signal:

The player can switch the effect in and out of the **signal path**, by simply pressing the **footswitch** on the stompbox. When it is off, or **bypassed**, the signal sounds the same as if the effect were not there. By joining effects together, either as a series of stompboxes or combined in a single **multi-effects unit**, it is possible to alter the signal with any number of effects at the same time. The results can be subtle textures or outrageous sounds, and can allow the instrument to take on a variety of different personalities at the press of a button.

Before we explore the exciting tonal possibilities of effects, let's introduce ourselves to the three most common formats for effects processors.

Effects Pedal

The **stompbox** is certainly the most common format and is a simple and cheap way to use effects. The circuitry is housed in a small metal box (cheaper units may have plastic casing), which features the **controls**, **in-out sockets**, a **battery compartment** and a **footswitch**. In some models this footswitch will be a heavy-duty "button" type; but more usually it is in the form of a large pad with the switch underneath. More modern stompboxes will also have an **LED indicator**—a small colored light that illuminates when the device is turned on, and an **AC adapter** socket that allows the unit to use a transformer instead of the internal battery. There are literally hundreds of effects pedals available, capable of creating a multitude of thrilling noises from within their funky colored cases. Stompboxes represent the fun side of effects processing and often have names to match. **Fuzz Face**, **Purple Platypus**, **Gonkulator** and **Meatball** are just some of the whacky monikers that keep effects from getting too serious.

The strong points of stompboxes are their portability, affordability and durability. Designed to withstand the rigors of being underfoot and small enough to keep in your guitar case, they make a lot of sense for players wanting a few simple effects. In addition, they can be linked together in an infinite number of ways to create some truly individual tones. The only drawback with this format is when a player wants to use a lot of different effects. As each stomp-box usually provides only one effect, a lot would be needed to cover a whole range of sounds. As well as being expensive, this also clutters your playing area with boxes and cables to trip over. Furthermore, the sound quality will suffer when the signal is patched through countless units and connecting cables. Stompbox users and abusers: Jimi Hendrix, Kurt Cobain, Joe Satriani, Jeff Beck and The Edge.

Floor-Mounted Multi-Effects

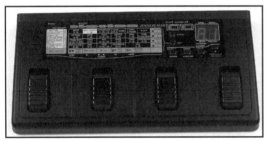

Floor units started when several companies combined a number of effects into a single large stompbox with separate switches for each effect. With time, and the wonders of technology, manufacturers were able to squeeze more and more sounds into these compact units. This is a fast-growing area of the effects market, with new variations being introduced regularly. These units range from small, inexpensive models to larger, professional systems, and there is plenty to choose from. By using discrete micro-chips and digital technology these units can produce virtually every effect in numerous combinations. Unlike stompboxes, they also have the advantage of being **programmable**, so when a particular sound has been constructed it can be stored as a **patch** in the unit's memory and recalled at any time. Cheaper models are compromised by having a limited control over the settings and the number of effects that can be used at once. However, some of the budget units offer an amazing number of programmable sounds for the cost of a single stompbox. The professional units benefit from a more

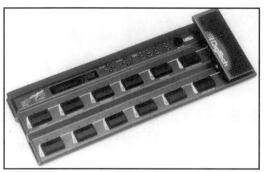

rugged metal casing
and have unlimited
control over the settings
and much larger memo-
ries. Floor unit users
and abusers: Dimebag
Darrell, Dominic Miller
(Sting) and Crispian
Mills (Kula Shaker).

Rack-Mounted Multi-Effects

This is very much the serious end of effects processing,
when space and money are not major considerations. Rack
units offer complete control over your sound with high-
powered processing of the type found in recording studios.
Unlike floor units, racks have the processor's brain in a
modular unit that is housed in a protective case, known as
a **rack**. A player can choose to use a single unit, or combine
any number for endless tonal variation. These devices are
also programmable and can be so complex that a computer
is required to control them. In most cases they are used
with a floor-based **foot controller**, which is a series of
footswitches mounted on a separate unit that is used to
access the sounds generated by the processors. Although
this can be an expensive and complex format for using
effects, a simple system can be assembled for a price compa-
rable to that of higher-range floor units. Rack effects users
and abusers: Steve Vai, Steve Lukather, Eddie Van Halen
and Reeves Gabrels (David Bowie).

A Tourist Guide to Multi-Effects

Before exploring the different effects available, it would be helpful to cover the basic structure and terminology of floor and rack multi-effects. As their name suggests, multi-effects link together many devices in a single unit, with various combinations stored as patches in the memory. These patches are subdivided into **banks**, accessible via a footswitch to select the bank and then patch. Moving through the patches within a bank may require using a pair of **up-down** footswitches. This is called **scrolling**. These switches are also used to adjust an effect's settings, or **parameters**. These systems usually come with two sets of patches: pre-programmed **factory presets** and programmable **user presets**. The user presets are used to store sounds you have created. This requires adjusting the parameters of different effects in the **edit mode**, then using a **save** or **store** button to save them as a user patch for future use. This may sound complicated but is actually a very simple process, especially if you take time to study the manual.

How They Work

For most of us, the electronic shenanigans that take place in the average effects unit make less sense than tax forms, and are probably equally as uninteresting. However, it is interesting to note that guitar effects use a bizarre collection of technologies to do what they do—from the unbelievably ancient to state-of-the-art. To this day, devices with mechanically rotating parts and moving loops of audiotape are still used alongside virtually obsolete components from the 1920s, microchips and powerful computer software. It seems that guitarists don't care how an effect is produced as long as it sounds good. In that rather eccentric frame of mind we'll look at an A-to-Z rundown of all the effects and concentrate on what they *sound* like. We won't attempt to tackle circuit diagrams and the finer points of audio physics. This should give you an idea of what to expect from an effects unit, and hopefully clear up some of the confusion surrounding their often misleading names.

Acoustic Simulator

This a relative newcomer to the world of effects and was pioneered by **Boss**, which is one of the biggest and most influential effects manufacturers. This effect takes the signal from an electric guitar and makes it sound uncannily like an acoustic guitar. By changing the round sustaining tone of an electric into the trademark snap and jangle of an acoustic, this pedal, or processor-based effect, is very realistic. Perfect for those acoustic intros when it's a pain to switch guitars.

18

Auto-Wah

This is an extremely funky device that first appeared in the '70s and really sounds like it. The auto-wah produces

the same vocal sounds of a **wah-wah** pedal (see the "wah-wah" description) but is triggered electronically rather than with a manu-ally operated **foot rocker**. The harder the guitar is played, the more the unit "wahs." The point at which this occurs is set by the **sensitivity** or **threshold** control. By adjusting the level of this control to your play-ing style, the effect can be triggered as you strum or pick slightly harder than normal. This is one fun effect that really runs the gamut. At its cheesiest, it puts you right in the middle of a *Starsky & Hutch* car chase; used more subtly, it adds an aquatic burbling to your tone.

Aural Exciter

This is not a strictly guitar-based effect but does appear in the form

of pedals and processor patches. Sometimes called an **aural**

19

enhancer, exciter or tone restorer, this subtle effect primarily adds a sweetening sheen to the overall tone. By boosting various frequencies, the device makes the guitar tone sound warmer, fatter and more detailed. It is especially useful when the signal becomes lackluster for players who use lots of effects, especially in the high frequencies, and helps to correct these losses. Aphex and BBE are two companies that specialize in this effect.

Booster

This is a term that isn't used by modern manufacturers but still appears on older and reissue pedals. Essentially, a booster boosts something—such as high frequencies (treble booster)—or makes the overall signal louder. Some effects

offer a clean boost, which simply ups the volume by a few notches without altering the sound. This is useful for guitar solos or other parts that need to rise above the backing instruments. As a booster amplifies the signal on its way to the amplifier itself it is also sometimes called a preamp.

Chorus

Pioneered by **Roland** in the '70s, the chorus was one of the first stand-alone electronic effects. Part of the closely related family of effects that includes **phasers**, **flangers** and

vibrato, the chorus also uses a **time-based cycle** to control the effect. It works by taking the signal and duplicating it with another that is slightly out of tune. This is set by the **depth** control and gives the guitar a thicker sound, as if two instruments are playing at once.

This effect is governed by the **rate** control, which produces a pulsing movement in the sound. With a low rate and low depth, the chorus adds a lush shimmer to the guitar sound. It can be quite subtle but produces a more interesting and sweeter tone, especially with clean sounds. With a high rate and high depth, the tone becomes a rich warble, not unlike the sound of a **Hammond** organ and very similar to the vibrato effect. This effect is often offered with a stereo option for an even larger sound.

Compressor

Maybe not the most dramatic effect, but certainly one of the most useful. Compressors are vital in recording studios but are also a useful addition to guitar setups in the form of pedals and processor patches. The main task of a compressor is to control the **dynamics** of the sound—how loud

things are in comparison to one another. A normal guitar signal jumps up and down as you play, from little peaks when single notes are played to big surges when an open chord is strummed hard. A compressor takes this signal and turns it into a uniform sound so that the output is even and smooth. A **threshold** control determines the volume to which the signals are pulled up, and can be adjusted to suit your playing style, allowing the effect to sound more natural. A mild compression tightens up the overall sound, particularly useful for techniques like fingerpicking that tend to sound jumpy. Higher levels of compression will add a noticeable amount of **sustain** (the time taken for a note to fade) and will allow smaller details like pick-scrapes, harmonics, etc., to sound as loud as chords. This is useful for complex lead playing where many different techniques are used, with the result being a smooth even tone. Compressors are a favorite of players who use a clean sound, as they add glossy punch and sustain to picked passages.

Delay

This is a dramatic and much used effect, and is often among the first effect purchases for guitar players. A delay takes the signal, duplicates it, then flings it back at you at a given rate—a controllable echo, in other words. This is governed by two controls: **feedback** and **delay time**. The first determines how many echos, or **repeats**, the effect produces, and the second governs the rate at which these repeats appear. With the time set high and the feedback low,

a single repeat appears just after the actual note is played. This is known as a **slap-back** delay and reproduces the sound of early rock 'n' rollers like Eddie Cochran. With the time set low and the feedback high, a series of distinct repeats is produced that can be played over, a technique used to dramatic effect by David Gilmour on Pink Floyd records. If the delay time is set to the tempo of the song, then these repeats take on a rhythmic role—a trademark sound of The Edge on early U2 albums. Between these extremes many ambient textures and impressive depths can be added to the guitar sound to produce moody rhythms and soaring solos. This is another effect that is often used in stereo for added drama; if the repeats alternate from one side to another it is called a **panning** or **ping-pong** delay.

Distortion

Possibly the most common of all effects, distortion appears in many guises and really epitomizes the sound of the electric guitar. Distortion originates from the sound produced when a guitar amplifier is pushed toward breaking point. The resulting tone is messed up in a very pleasing way, and different degrees of distortion yield different tones, from the warm sizzle of blues to the crunch of rock to the aggressive grind of metal. These are all forms of distortion. This phenomenon was reproduced as an effect so that these sought-after sounds could be achieved without forcing amps

toward melt-down, or so that even more distortion could be added to an already cooking sound. While most players agree on what a good delay sounds like, distortion is as personal as your under-pants. For this reason there are countless distortion devices available in every format, from the tame to the positively terrifying. This also makes it difficult to define, as the term encompasses other effects such as **overdrive** and **fuzz**. However, it is generally accepted that distortion is the more extreme end of **dirty** (i.e., not clean) tones, producing the raucous sounds associated with rock, punk and metal bands.

Detuner

A detuner is a similar effect to the chorus, but without a time-based cycle. The guitar signal is duplicated with another that is slightly detuned to produce a thicker sound. This process "humanizes" the guitar sound to emulate the slight difference in tuning when two guitarists play together. For this reason the effect is also known as doubling. Although uncommon in pedal form, it often appears in floor and rack-mounted processors.

Echo

Before the advent of the delay, the only way to produce an echo effect was with a machine the size of a microwave that used loops of audiotape to duplicate and play back the

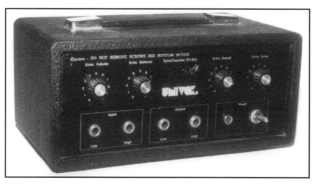

signal. These cumber- some devices were burdened with prob- lems other than size.

The noisy tape loops would wear out and need replacing regularly, or simply snap mid-performance. Most players were happy to switch to the reliable and compact delay pedals that replaced them, but some folk missed the warm fluttery sound of the tape-driven "echo chambers." Sought-after models such as the **Watkins Copicat** and **Echoplex** are still used today, either as modern replicas or vintage collector's items. However, most players prefer to replicate these sounds with modern effects. The echo effect is available as pedals, processor patches and even dedicated rack units. Unlike the clean powerful sound of digital delays, these circuits emulate the warmer, more gloopy sound of tape units associated with early "pop" bands like the Shadows. Featuring the same controls as a digital delay (feedback, delay time), some units, like the **DOD FX96 Echo** pedal, also incorporate a **quality** control to mimic the distortion produced from worn-out tape loops.

Ducking

Nothing to do with Chuck Berry, this effect appears on the more advanced effects processors as a means of making various patches sound more natural when moving from one to another. For example, if you are playing with a delay then move to a patch without delay, the repeats continue to fade away naturally over the new sound, instead of stopping abruptly.

Envelope Follower

This is not strictly an effect, but a device that is capable of controlling effects through the dynamics of your playing. The harder the guitar is picked, the more the envelope follower increases the attached effect, resulting in a sound that responds to the player's technique. By far the most common use of this device is in the auto-wah, (see "Auto-wah" explanation) which is why they are sometimes incorrectly described as envelope followers. Although this device is not usually offered as a stand-alone foot pedal, it appears in a number of multi-effects units combined with other effects (such as flanging or phasing, where it controls the rate).

EQ

These two little letters stand for **equalization** and mean a whole lot. Any sound is made up from a range of **frequencies**. When a guitar string is plucked, it produces only one note, but that sound is made up from lots of other sounds that produce that specific tone—which is why one guitar sounds different from another, and why they all sound different from a bassoon playing the same note. Confused? Okay, if you think of the note as being dark purple, then the frequencies are the different amounts of red, blue and black that mix together and make that note. The job of the EQ is to separate these "colors" and adjust their mix, thereby altering the tone— i.e., to make a *different* dark purple.

This effect can be simply called a **tone control**, like the bass,

middle and treble knobs on an amplifier, or **tone** controls on an effect unit. However, their power to dramatically shape sound has produced many dedicated devices. One is the **parametric EQ**, which allows specific areas of frequencies to be selected, then exaggerated or removed—known as a **cut** or **boost**. These are normally left to sound engineers, as they require nimble finger work. A more common format for guitarists is a **graphic EQ**. These use **slider** controls for each group of frequencies (from three to as many as 32 in a dedicated rack unit), so-called because the position of the sliders gives a graphic view of the tone's shape—you can see which parts are cut or boosted. A graphic EQ may be used in the form of a pedal, manipulated via the display window of a processor, or as a separate rack unit.

E-Bow

This is something of an oddball as it is a hand-held effect that isn't plugged into the guitar or amp. The E-Bow is held in the picking hand and brought near the strings, where the battery-driven electro-  magnetic circuitry causes the strings to vibrate, giving rise to eerie violinlike swells. In recent years this technology has also been built into guitars; the **Sustainer** system offered on **Fernandes** guitars is a popular version. In this case the device is fitted into part of the neck pickup and can be switched on as required.

Flanger

This effect first appeared in recording studios when two tapes of the same recording were played simultaneously and the engineer slowed one down by dragging a finger against it. The small delay caused the trademark whooshing sound

as the two sets of frequencies moved against one another. By the '70s this effect could be duplicated electronically, the stompbox flanger mimicking the inter-tape weirdness. Modern flangers split the signal, then apply a short delay over a timed cycle, like its relative the chorus, and also features **depth** and **rate** controls. In addition, many flangers have a **resonance** control, which adds interesting metallic overtones—turn it way up and you get a fair impression of a steel drum! The thick swoosh of a flanger is easy to spot. Check out Van Halen's "And The Cradle Will Rock" intro for this classic sound.

Fuzz

The fuzz is a distortion device that first appeared in the 1960s and rocked the guitar world with its raw, dangerous sound. Unlike modern distortion units, the fuzz uses only a handful of components to produce its unrefined, rasping buzz—a case of attitude over sound quality.

It became one of the most popular effects, largely due to Jimi Hendrix, who rarely performed without one. The model he favored was the **Arbiter Fuzz Face,** which is still made today by the **Jim Dunlop** company. This cool, flying-saucer-shaped stompbox coaxes frazzled violinlike tones from excited amps, perfect for nostalgic solos. Many other

famous "fuzz boxes" appeared in the 1960s, like the **Mayer Axis Fuzz**, which was also shaped like a spaceship and used by Hendrix. These and others, like the **Electro-Harmonix Big Muff**, are also still available. The effect is also common in multi-effects processors and as an optional setting on some modern distortion pedals.

Graphic EQ

See "EQ" description.

Harmonizer

This effect came to the forefront in the 1980s and became the plaything of many technical rock guitarists. The harmonizer, or **pitch shifter**, allows the guitar signal to be duplicated with another of a different pitch, giving the impression that two guitars are playing in harmony. In its simplest form the second signal is played an octave higher or lower, called an **octaver**, but harmonizers can also play many other **intervals**. A standard interval can be chosen (e.g., a fifth), the resulting sound being pleasing, dense and complex, again sounding like two guitarists playing at once. More unusual intervals can be used to create thick dissonant sounds—think incidental music in horror movies. One problem with early harmonizers arose from the interval being fixed, whereas in true harmonies the interval would need to change to make certain notes correct. The answer came with **intelligent harmonizers**, which can work out when the chosen interval needs to move and correct various notes. These are available in pedal form such as the **Boss HR-2 Harmonist**, in multi-effects like the **Rocktron Intellifex** rack unit, or as super-brainy rack units like the **Eventide H3000 Harmonizer**.

Leslie Speaker

This is a truly crazy device that appeared in a time before electronics were used extensively in guitar effects. This mechanical monster consisted of a large cabinet containing a revolving speaker attached to an electric motor. The output from the amplifier is attached to the unit and the speed of the motor can be altered to your liking. The resulting noise from the spinning speakers is a thick, shimmering warble, not unlike the sound of a chorus. This is because it actually works on the same principle, with part of the signal being slightly detuned over a time-based cycle, except this time it uses the doppler effect—a physical phenomenon where sound appears to drop in pitch as the source moves away from the listener, and the reason why the siren on an ambulance seems to get lower as it passes. These large and heavy units have largely been replaced by chorus-type effects, although a few models are still made for players seeking that authentic tone. **Mesa Engineering** produces a modern example. However, with the recent rekindling of interest in vintage effects, many companies have begun to offer **Leslie-emulation** effects—an electronic version of the old mechanical unit. There are a number of pedal versions of this effect as well. The **Jim Dunlop UV-1** and the **Hughes & Kettner RotoSphere** are two examples, but it is also a common inclusion in floor and rack multi-effects.

Limiter

Limiters are often confused with compressors, but they are not entirely the same effect. A compressor "pulls" the signal up to the volume set by the threshold. A limiter "pushes" the signal down to the volume set by the threshold. This may seem like a subtle difference, but is really one that has a very different effect on the dynamics of the sound. Careful application of compression or limiting is very useful for preventing unwanted peaks and jumps while playing, and especially while recording. These units are a mainstay in recording studios.

Sometimes the two different effects are combined for more powerful sound control. These combination units are simply called **compressor/limiters**. They also appear as pedals and rack units, or in multi-effects boxes.

Modeling

As the digital technology used in guitar effects and amplifiers becomes increasingly powerful, companies have been able to achieve what was once considered impossible. Modeling is one such area of signal processing that has brought about some dramatic changes in guitar effects. Essentially, sought-after sounds, such as the tone of rare vintage amps, can be converted into a digital model—a "virtual" amp that sounds and behaves like the real thing.

33

As digital processors can store a lot of information they are capable of replicating the tone of a garageful of vintage amps and effects in different combinations. This type of

effect is usually found in amplifiers, such as those made by **Line 6**, **Johnson** and **Yamaha**, but also appears in rack formats like **Yamaha's DG 1000** unit. The most advanced of these systems use special digital, or **hexaphonic**, pickups that must be attached to the guitar. This gives the player even more control of the sound and can be used to control guitar-based **synthesizers** like the **Roland VG-8**.

Noise Gate

This device, also known as a **silencer**, removes unwanted noise from the signal, leaving complete silence when the

instrument is not being played. A **threshold** control sets the level for noises allowed to pass through the device (i.e., the actual signal from the guitar) and any below the threshold are silenced, including background hum, buzzing, lead crackles and handling noises. It literally operates like a gate, opening to let the sound of the instrument through, but remaining closed to irritating background noises. These are available in all formats, but **noise reduction** is a more common inclusion for multi-effects units. A noise reduction circuit does not open or close, but filters out the frequencies common to background noises, like the **Dolby** circuitry in stereo systems. **Rocktron's Hush** unit is a popular example of a complex filter of this type.

Octaver

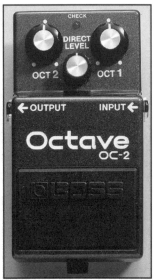

Octavers were the very first pitch shifters and appeared in the 1960s. This effect duplicates the guitar's main signal with another sound an octave lower. It was yet another effect favored by Jimi Hendrix. The result is almost like hearing a guitar and bass play the same thing—particularly impressive for fast runs.

Later versions of this effect produced an octave above the original note, producing a sound similar to a 12-string guitar, and sometimes both at once for a truly orchestrated tone. Octavers are readily available as pedals by **Boss, DOD, MXR, Roger Mayer**, etc., but be warned that some of these are combined with a fuzz tone, so be sure to seek out one that suits your application. This effect is also common within the patches of harmonizers and multi-effects.

Overdrive

This effect is another variation on the distortion theme and is generally used to describe the soft, creamy distortion produced by hard-pushed vintage tube amplifiers. Unlike gain-laden aggressive distortions, overdrive is more restrained and warmer sounding, a tone often favored by blues players. As with any distortion effect, there are count-less variations on the market, from pedals to dedicated processors and everything in between. Some popular pedal models include the **Ibanez TS-9 Tubescreamer**, the **Tube Works Tube Driver** and the **Marshall Guvnor**.

Panning

If effects are run in stereo (left and right), then one channel usually plays the uneffected, or **dry**, signal and the other channel the sound with the effect, or the **wet** signal. This gives a more complex sound with greater dimension. A panning effect is used to liven things up even further by sweeping the wet and dry signals across the two channels, giving a sense of movement as the effected sound moves from one side to the other. In this way the panning control is used only in combination with stereo effects and, as such, is uncommon as a stompbox-type unit. More commonly it appears as an option in multi-effects menus, or combined with another effect in stereo stompboxes such as some modern delay and tremolo pedals.

Phaser

Not quite the same thing that was wielded by Spock and Captain Kirk, but it can be set to stun. Also known as a **phase shifter**, this device belongs to the same family as the chorus and flanger and has a similar range of sounds. The phase shifter operates by removing a chunk from the guitar's signal frequencies and sweeping it up and down over a time-based cycle. In this way the chunk is taken from a different part of the frequency range as the phaser

moves through the cycle, at a speed determined by the **rate** control. At higher rates the sound is similar to the chorus or Leslie effect; at slower speeds it sounds much like a flanger but with a less pronounced "whoosh." The signal can be heard moving between muted, bass-heavy tones, to bright, treble-based sounds, adding a watery movement to the sound of the guitar. In the early days of effects, the terms "phasing" and "flanging" were often used interchangeably, but modern devices make the difference more apparent. Phasers are useful for adding interesting textures to guitar passages when a chorus is too subtle and a flanger would be too dominant. There are many versions of this effect found in multi-effects and pedals. Some historically important stompbox phasers include the **MXR Phase 90** (used by Eddie Van Halen on many early recordings) and the retro-approved **Electro-Harmonix Small Stone**. Both of these units are still living quite prosperously.

Pitch Shifter

A pitch shifter, or **pitch transposer**, basically takes a

signal and alters the **pitch** being played—you

play one note, it turns it into another. However, as the shifted note is normally played together with the original note, these devices are usually classified as harmonizers. (Refer to the "harmonizer" section for more information on these devices.)

Preamp

The term preamp covers many things in the sphere of guitars, which can be very confusing. In general terms, a

preamp is a small amplifier that boosts the guitar signal on its way to the main amplifier; it may also shape the sound with EQ controls. The different types of preamp are categorized by where they are found. If the preamp is contained in the guitar itself (electric or electro-acoustic) it will be a discreet, battery-powered unit capable of boosting the signal, usually with some form of EQ for tone control. This is called an **active** preamp. If it is part of a guitar amplifier, it is the section that comes before the main **power amp** that is responsible for shaping the sound and usually includes **gain** (amount of amp distortion) and **tone** (EQ) controls. In terms of effects, it can mean several

different things—just to add to the confusion! In its simplest form it will be a pedal, like the booster described earlier, that offers an additional amount of gain or volume. More complex pedals, like the **Tech 21 SansAmp,** will include distortion and EQ functions. **Rack-mounted preamps** are used with separate power amps in place of a normal guitar amplifier to produce a large range of different tones—these will contain a comprehensive EQ section and different types of clean and distorted sounds. As many of these rack-mounted preamps include effects too, the term "preamp" is also used as generic term to describe multi-effects units in general.

Reverb

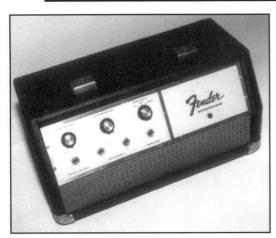

This vibrant effect was first introduced on early guitar amplifiers and has remained a common addition to many modern amps. Using a bizarre circuit based around long springs, the **spring** reverb is capable of adding a small delay to the signal that allows the previous note to continue over the one being played. Although not as pronounced as an echo, this effect still adds a dramatic sense of space to the sound—as if you are playing in a large hall instead of your bedroom. For players without a built-in reverb on their amps, spring reverb was available as an add-on effect, sometimes called a **reverb chamber**, which is about the size of a small amplifier **head**. Although these effects are still manufactured and used today, the bulky items were mostly replaced by **digital reverbs,** which are available in the much more practical form of a pedal, rack or multi-effects unit. Using the same technology as delay effects, electronic reverbs can mimic the inspiring sound of the original spring-driven effect and often use terms such as **small room**, **large hall**, etc., as a reference to the depth of the effect.

Ring Modulator

This is another of those weird funky effects that appeared

in the '70s, when guitarists were hungry for any type of freaky sound. This is an ugly-sounding effect that is best used sparingly for occasional atonal fun and is not one of the most popular sounds ever devised. The ring modulator produces a selectable signal of its own, combines that with the guitar signal, then delivers two completely different mathematically related signals— which sound as horrible as you would expect.

It is a perfect effect for momentary insanity and to take your audience by surprise. This effect also occasionally appears in multi-effects units and crusty old stompboxes.

Speaker Emulator

This device appears in many multi-effects units and preamps, and is a useful recording tool. To capture the sound of the electric guitar in a studio requires using one or more microphones and an amp—a loud and time-consuming process. The speaker emulator cuts out this part of recording by mimicking the effect of the signal passing through speakers and microphones. This makes recording faster, quieter and easier, and, although professional studios still prefer the authentic sound of a miked amp, people recording at home really benefit from this hassle-free system. Although speaker emulators are normally found in multi-effects units, there are some stompbox-style preamps that offer this effect in a compact package. Check out the **Tech 21 SansAmp** and **Session** pedals.

Sustain

This term describes the length of time a note takes to fade away; a sustain effect is designed to increase this time. This

is really an outdated name that used to cover both compressors and distortion effects; however, these two effects are very different and are now referred to by those names. Sustain itself is determined by many factors, including the actual guitar and playing technique, and while various effects can help a note hang around longer, none of them will produce convincing sustain from a dead plank of a guitar or fluffy playing.

Sampler

Samplers were introduced as an effect in dance music, where they could copy a short piece of sound (a drum pattern, guitar riff, breaking glass, roadie burp, etc.) and play it back as required. Phrases could be **looped** and played continuously as a backing track, or the sample could be controlled via a keyboard and reproduced at different pitches. (Oh, how we almost laughed at Beethoven's Fifth played as armpit noises.) Comedy hit singles aside, the sampler has become a powerful performance tool for many musicians, including guitar players. Essentially a powerful delay effect, it is often found in multi-effects and some pedals as part of the delay options. A short phrase can be recorded (**sampled**) then either played back as a continuous loop, or **triggered** in some way, such as using a **drum machine**—which allows the phrase to sound at a predetermined rate. This guitar effect is often heard on dance and industrial metal records.

Tremolo

This is another effect that made its debut in guitar amps and found a place in the nostalgic heart of guitarists. Often confused with **vibrato** (including being misnamed on amps and effects), the tremolo is a time-based device along the lines of chorus and Leslie effects. The signal is basically turned on and off at an adjustable rate, and this effect normally has just a single **rate** control. This produces a range of sounds from a slow pulse to a fast stutter, sounding similar to a Leslie effect but less fluid. This effect has enjoyed a recent comeback and can be found in all effect formats and some amplifiers. If the rate is matched to the tempo of the song, the pulsed signal plays in time with the music to dramatic effect.

Talk Box

This freak of the effects world involves using a body orifice—sticking a tube in your mouth. Sounding more like an alien abduction procedure than a musical device, the talk box is actually a very cool effect. The device itself is very simple but requires other equipment to operate. The guitar signal travels to the talk box, where it is split, with one

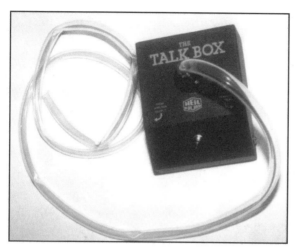

signal traveling on to the guitar amp and another to a small amp contained in the talk box. This internal amp drives a small speaker that forces the sound up through a plastic tube. This tube is attached to a vocal microphone, which itself must be amplified through another amp or **PA system**. The player can then use his or her mouth to shape the sound of the signal coming through the tube, which is then picked up by the microphone. With practice, the guitar can sound eerily close to the human voice, hence "talk box." Certainly not the easiest effect to use for many reasons, it is

capable of producing some highly unusual and original tones. It is often associated with guitarist Peter Frampton but also known to many through Bon Jovi's "Livin' on a Prayer" hit single. One of the original manufacturers, **Heil**, still produces talk boxes, and collectable original models are much in demand, such as the **Electro-**

Harmonix Golden Throat and **Kustom's The Bag**. This was the first commercially available talk box and it looked like a psychedelic bagpipe!

Uni-Vibe

Originally produced by the **Univox** company, this effect combines a phaser and vibrato to produce some fine psychedelic tone-wobbling. The rate at which the effect operates can be altered using a **foot rocker** (a flat pad not unlike a car's gas pedal), the speed increasing as the pedal is pushed down. This unusual combination produces some expressive swirling tones and is another effect associated with Jimi Hendrix. Often used to describe patches in multi-effects, this device is also still available as various pedals from companies such as **Jim Dunlop**, **Prescription Electronics** and **VooDoo Lab**.

Vibrato

As mentioned previously, this effect is often confused with tremolo but is actually closer to chorus in its sound and operation. Vibrato causes the guitar signal to waver slightly in and out of tune over a cycle set by the **rate** control, and a **depth** control determines how much the signal is pulled out of tune. Vibrato's creamy warble is close to a Leslie effect, but less refined than chorus, and is a much-loved retro effect that is also common on vintage-style amplifiers. This effect is generally produced with chorus or phasers, but still appears in effects patches and amps.

Volume

Although everybody is familiar with a volume control, when used as an effect it can be surprisingly interesting. The **volume pedal** consists of little more than a volume control attached to a foot rocker, which allows the level to be increased as the pedal is pushed down. This can be used to fade in a guitar sound to achieve subtle keyboard textures, or used with single notes for violinlike swells. Used in conjunction with other effects like delay and chorus, this simple device can produce some very convincing synthesizer tones. It also makes a highly practical master volume control for complex setups, so the overall volume can be adjusted or turned off as needed. Most effects companies offer stand-alone volume pedals or include them in floor-based effects units.

Wah-Wah

Perhaps a silly name, but it perfectly describes the sound of this hugely popular effect. This device contains a filter that sweeps through the frequencies of the guitar tone and is controlled with a foot rocker pedal. This is a highly expressive effect that adds vowel-like sounds to the guitar, producing the trademark "wah" when the pedal is pressed. As the effect is controlled by the player it can be used to exaggerate phrases—single notes or rhythms—adding a sense of speed, movement and downright funkiness. This effect has appeared on zillions of recordings. Hendrix is considered one of its greatest proponents, but it has been used by everyone from Aerosmith to Zappa. The human quality of this effect has certainly helped its popularity and it remains one of the most enjoyed effects to this day. Often offered as an optional sound on floor-based effects equipped with rocker pedals, the preferred format is the original pedal design. **Jim Dunlop**, **Morley** and **Vox** produce some of the most popular models.

Whammy

Introduced by the **DigiTech** company, this foot-controlled pitch shifter is extremely popular. The Whammy allows the pitch of the guitar to be altered with a wah-style rocker pedal, enabling a note or chord to be bent up to two octaves higher than the original signal. It can dramatically sweep chords into the stratosphere, transpose entire sections of music to other keys or octaves, or add some serious squeals to lead playing. This effect has been used by many modern rock players including Joe Satriani, Steve Vai and Dimebag Darrell. It is available as the original **DigiTech Whammy**, or in a number of other DigiTech effects units.

Different Types

Thus far we have established that there are three formats for effects, and we know how each effect behaves and sounds. At this point it would seem useful to look at some other fundamental differences in the types of effects offered. This will help clear up some of the terminology that is thick in the air of guitar stores, and give you more of an idea of what to expect from specific products.

Vintage Versus Modern

In the last chapter many of the effects were described as being vintage or modern, largely to explain their position in the effect evolutionary chain. However, if you are to walk into a music store, there will be all manner of effects sitting in that glass case under the counter because, like most guitar technologies, the old are not discarded in favor of the new, they are simply added on. In the beginning, older effects were superseded by new designs that were more reliable, more powerful and quieter. In time, many guitarists began to miss the squelchy sounds and eccentric behavior

of some of these early effects. As pawn shops and classifieds were scoured for these discarded oddities, the second-hand pedal market became the vintage pedal market, and now originals fetch collector's prices.

Effects manufacturers were quick to realize the potential of their old designs, which seemed to generate as much interest

as their state-of-the-art products, and began to make them again. These historically authentic effects are called **reissues**, and companies like DOD sell their '60s and '70s designs alongside their brand-new versions. Bizarrely, an original vintage pedal may sell for as much as three times the cost of a new reissue, with a modern version often costing even less—crazy but true. If you seek powerful, efficient effects, then modern products are probably the answer. If, however, you wish to recreate the sounds of classic players, then it is worth trying some of the excellent reissues now available. Due to the cost of originals, not to mention they could well be older than you (which isn't a benefit for electronic devices), these collector's items are best left to the collector's them-selves, being too expensive and fragile to use regularly.

If, like many players, you want to use a mixture of modern and vintage effects, then it is worth knowing that some products combine the two. For example, the **Boss FZ-2 Hyper Fuzz** is a new pedal capable of producing vintage fuzz tones and modern distortions. On a larger scale, many multi-effect

units include patches that reproduce authentic fuzz, Leslie and tremolo sounds, among others.

Analog Versus Digital

Here is another pair of terms often used to distinguish effects. Essentially, the earliest effects used old **analog** electronics in their design, whereas modern effects often use digital circuits. Rather than swamp ourselves in the physics of these two technologies, it is easier to describe them in terms of sound.

Analog circuits are less powerful and efficient compared with digital versions. Delays are shorter, ranges are limited and the effects are not as clean or crisp in their operation. But analog devices sound warm, organic and sometimes more interesting than their digital counterparts, which explains the popularity of vintage effects. Furthermore, digital circuits are actually unsuitable for producing certain effects—many digital

distortions were considered cacophonous failures (although huge improvements in modeling have dispelled this). As a result, effects manufacturers now use both analog and digital circuits to offer the best of both sounds, often combined in the same product. In this way the technologies complement each other. Powerful, complex effects are performed by digital circuits, and analog steps in for vintage sounds and added warmth.

Synths and Software

On the subject of digital technology, it would be an oversight to ignore the increasing role of the computer in guitar processing. As computer technology gets faster and more affordable, the household PC is becoming increasingly useful to guitar players. The use of computer modeling has already been covered, and the Roland VG-8 synth system is

a staggering testimony to what this technology can achieve. However, the humble PC is fast overtaking these expensive effects systems with the arrival of affordable software. This rapidly expanding area of home computing offers some exciting prospects for mouse-savvy guitarists. By connecting your guitar directly to your computer, even without a digital pickup, it is possible to create and record a boggling array of guitar sounds. In addition to being a superb learning tool, this technology also brings high-quality home recording to the masses. Companies like **Cakewalk** produce guitar-oriented software packages for recording and arranging music, and effects software capable of generating a studio's worth of effects from a single CD-ROM. If you intend to try recording and can stumble around a PC, then be sure to check out these exciting products.

Buyer's Guide

5.

FRESH Effects

FUZZ BOX | PHASE SHIFTER | WAH-WAH | BASS DISTORTI

If you are thinking about buying effects, then it's safe to assume you already own a guitar and amp. Your amp is a good place to start when considering which effects to buy, as its design will have a bearing on your choices. First of all, you need to decide what you like about the tones you already have. Most amps have two channels, one for distortion and the other for clean sound. If you really like these sounds then you will want to concentrate on effects that add texture rather than change the actual tone of the amp, like distortion or EQ effects. If you are unhappy with the tone of your amp then you need to investigate products that can produce the distorted and clean sounds you want.

If you are thinking of using time-based effects, like chorus, flanging and especially delay, then an **effects loop** is a real benefit on your amp. This appears as a pair of sockets marked **send** and **return**, with allow your effects to be connected after the distortion section of the amp (send goes into effects, output from effects is connected to return). The reason being that some of these effects can sound lumpy and noisy if used before distortion. If you don't have an effects loop then you can choose to ignore the amp-based distortion and use a separate pedal or multi-effect patches for dirty tones.

Finally, you need to decide how many effects you wish to use, which brings us to the stompbox multi-effects dilemma. Stompboxes are robust, interchangeable and simple to use, while offering complete control over the settings of an individual effect. However, every time a pedal is introduced into the signal path a small amount of noise creeps in and a small amount of frequencies creep out. With a handful of pedals

56

this is not a noticeable problem, but if you intend to use 15 different effects then your tone will suffer, not to mention that your floor will look like the spilled innards of a space shuttle. Furthermore, compared with multi-effects, stomp-boxes stop making financial sense after a four or five units, as multi-effects offer more effects for less outlay. So multi-effects can provide heaps of effects for an affordable amount, but there are certain compromises.

First, finding your way around the programming and patches takes some manual reading; multi-effects are less obvious to operate than stomp-and-go pedals. Second, on budget models, the settings may not be as tweakable as stompboxes—there is often a small number of fixed settings rather than the infinite variation offered by a rotary control. Third, multi-effects are designed to generate an entire range of tones, which means that the models tend to have a signature sound of their own, a sort of inherent flavor that colors all the sounds and may overwhelm the tone of the amp. For example, if you have set up your amp with your favorite dirty sound and then try to use a multi-effect, the sound will be dramatically altered—distortion patches will be too dirty, and clean patches distorted. The solution is to use your amp with a clean, flat sound and rely on the effects for all tones, or to reprogram the patches to work with your chosen dirty and clean amp sounds. The point is that multi-effect processors can be bullies when it comes to amps, which is fine if you like their tones; otherwise they need to be taken in hand with some tough patch editing.

Budget

Before giving your credit card even a thoughtful glance, take it upon yourself to really listen to any effects you are thinking of buying. The best way to do this is to set aside some time and take your favorite guitar to a well-stocked music store. Ask if they have the model of amp you use in stock; if they don't, get permission to tote yours along—they should oblige. The reason for this is that effects respond differently to different guitars and amps. That wah-wah may sound fat with the store's Les Paul and Marshall, but scratchy and irritating with your own Strat and Fender Twin. Furthermore, although we've covered the basic sounds of each effect, there are so many variations that the same effect can sound very different depending on the model and manufacturer.

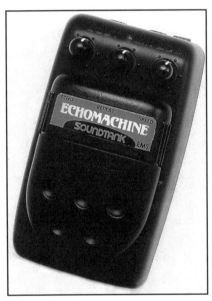

Budget really boils down to what you actually need. If you just want a couple of effects that you intend to use a lot, then aim for good-quality stompboxes. It is better to buy one sweet-sounding, robust stompbox than two fizzy, plastic-cased cheapos. With cheap units it's really a race between your getting sick of the low-quality sound and the units' falling apart; both are obviously undesirable. You can always add to your pedal collection as you can afford to. If you want to explore the outer limits of guitar effects then check out any of the multi-effects units. Budget models offer incredible bang for the buck, allowing many effects to be used at once with programmability and reasonable sound quality. They may not be as durable as stompboxes, but for coming to grips with all types of effects you could do plenty worse, and there is always the option to upgrade when you leave the bedroom for Carnegie Hall.

Manufacturers that produce affordable multi-effect units include **Zoom**, **DOD**, **Boss** and **Korg**.

If you have a healthy budget and pine for processing power, then any of the pro-level floor systems should be at top of your tryouts. Manufacturers like **Boss**, **Rocktron** and **DigiTech** all make some very powerful multi-effect models in metal "road-ready" cases with added rocker pedals for controlling wah, pitch-shifting and other effects. Programming allows a high level of tweakability, with many combinations of effects available at once and a large memory for storing patches. If this still seems like a compromise, then buckle up and head to the rack section. Although racks can be used to put together a cost-effective effects/amp system, their real power lies in being able to do everything short of solving the meaning of life. Starting with an empty case, you can fill it with dedicated preamp modules and effects processors until any conceivable tone is available through a MIDI-controlled pedal board. This is as technical as effects get, so be sure to seek professional advice and spend some serious

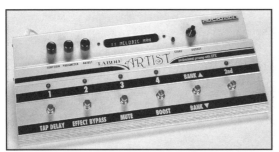

time in the store's sound room before making a costly commitment. The above companies, along with

Alesis, TC Electronics, Eventide, Marshall, Mesa Engineering, Yamaha, Roland, Soldano, etc., all produce pro-level rack-mount preamps and effects.

Used Equipment

For many novice guitarists, there isn't much left in the cookie jar to spend on effects after buying a guitar and amp. In this case, buying used equipment can make a lot of sense, as long as you are aware of the pitfalls. In this instance we are dealing with used but fairly current models, not those rusty old vintage pedals from '69 that cost more than your guitar. Used effects seem to sell for about half their new retail price, but be sure to try before you buy as it may not be obvious if that shiny pedal ever spent time at the bottom of a swimming pool or endured some similar disaster. If a device looks like it's been in several bar fights, chances are it won't be feeling too good on the inside either, and wouldn't make a sensible purchase.

Test all of the controls to make sure they are working and crackle-free. Run through all the patches on multi-effects units and check that any programming and editing functions work as they should. If the device can be battery-operated, flip open the cover and check for nasty brown gunk—this means a battery leaked and may have damaged the circuitry. If the device is sensitive to taps or vibrations and cuts out or thumps through the amp, then a loose circuit is going to make it a bad buy. If there is a noticeable amount of hum, buzzing or background noise, then the unit may not be properly screened and could be dangerous or at least annoying to use. If you have bought a used effect that misbehaves, get it checked out by a repairman. *Faulty effects can damage your amp and may be dangerous. Don't take the risk*!

If you intend to buy or sell privately, either through ads or the Internet, please be very careful. Establish beforehand exactly what it is you're buying, the price and any other details. Always send gear and checks by registered courier to minimize risks, and use common sense to protect yourself as much as possible.

Danger Will Robinson!

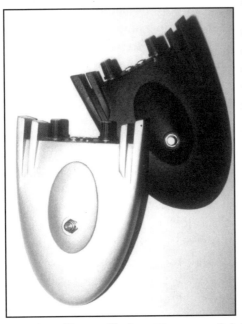

We'll cover the serious safety considerations later in the chapter, but here we'll look at the less-fatal dangers of Acquisition Frenzy. Anyone faced with a storeful of effects gets struck by AF: the urge to purchase at least one of every type. If you've never experienced a flanger before, chances are you'll immediately want one, along with a multi-effects offering 73 types of delay, a Supersquid Fibrillator, the Odin Octoburp and that thing in the corner that goes "ping." In other words, it's very easy to get carried away and come home with something that you use incessantly for three days, then stash under the bed, where it gathers dust for the rest of eternity. Effects can be very inspiring, but it is important to choose those that you will actually use. Certain effects become the mainstay in players' setups, distortion, delay, chorus, compressor and wah-wah being good examples. While more unusual or dramatic effects like flangers, harmonizers or talk boxes are fun to use, they are best used sparingly. To avoid wasting money on effects, stick with what you know you will use, as you can always add to them later. Hey, do you really need that refrigerator-sized mega-rack to thump out "Hotel California" at Uncle Bernie's retirement party?

Essential Checklist

You've got the cash, you've got the effects system of your dreams in sigh ... but let's just go back over the essential checks first, so you don't shoot yourself in the foot:

☐ Controls

Rotary controls, footswitches, rocker pedals and buttons should all perform positively without crackles or pops. On programmable units, check that all the edit functions operate as they should and check the memory by writing a patch, storing it, then retrieving and using it after the device has been turned off.

☐ Connections

Check that all connections (input/output sockets, AC cord, adapter sockets, etc.) are not loose, noisy or sensitive to use. If any cut out or thump then they could cause damage to the amplifier.

☐ Noise

Any effects unit should operate with a minimum of background noise. Loud buzzing, crackling or humming could indicate bad grounding or a loose connection. In any of these cases the unit could be dangerous and should be checked by a repairman.

☐ Battery Compartment

Especially important for used pedals; check the battery compartment for any signs of leaked acid. This noxious goo can destroy delicate components and the device should be checked before use.

☐ Paperwork

Before buying any device, ensure that it has the correct

manual (essential for complex multi-effects) and any warranty cards. Ask if the store has a return policy in case you are not happy with your purchase, and also whether they have any sort of warranty for used equipment. Replacement manuals for used effects can often be obtained from the manufacturer.

If all the above check out fine, then hand over the cash, head home and enjoy your effects.

Maintenance 6.

Unlike guitars, effects need little maintenance, unless you own a vintage mechanical device like a tape echo, in which case you can consult with your vintage dealer. Stompboxes, multi-effects and foot controllers live under our feet, which can be a very messy place. In order to combat footwear-related grunge, any underfoot devices should be given a regular wipe with a dampened soft cloth. Don't be tempted to spray domestic cleaning products on effect units; the mist may reach the circuit board and the chemicals can cause corrosion. Whenever you are not using your effects, keep them covered to prevent dust from gumming up the moving parts and circuitry. When you unwrap your new effects units, keep the boxes. Not only are they good for storing seldom-used effects and their manuals, but in years to come they may add to the resale value.

Perhaps the most important maintenance concerns battery-driven effects. Any device that uses a battery will drain the power when the **input** socket is connected, even if the device is turned off. Always ensure that the input of battery-operated effects is unplugged when not in use, or you'll go through Duracells as fast as an Yngwie Malmsteen arpeggio. More importantly, never leave batteries in an effect for a prolonged period as they may leak and perma-nently damage the circuitry. If you haven't used a pedal for a while, remove the battery before it can do any harm.

Safety Considerations

The safety concerns of effects units are the same for any electrically operated device: to keep the operator from exposure to the AC supply. The basic rules are simple:

1. Always use a **grounded** supply—*never* be tempted to break off the ground pin on three-pronged plugs.

2. Use a **circuit breaker** on all AC-powered equipment. These inexpensive devices go between the AC cord and wall socket, and will shut down the device at the first sign of electrical trouble. One of the best investments a musician can make.

3. Always replace any blown power fuses with those of the correct value (fuses are found in holders usually located on the rear panel of the unit). If the unit continues to blow fuses, have it checked.

4. If a unit is exposed to moisture, such as a spilled drink, turn it off *immediately* and have it checked by a repairman.

5. If the unit cuts out, buzzes, hums loudly or thumps in use, then a short could have occurred. This can be very dangerous, and also needs to be checked by a qualified repairman.

This all may seem like common sense, but people still risk using faulty equipment, and some have paid the ultimate price. The above guidelines cover any device that has an AC cord; let's now look at some more specific safety measures.

Most stompboxes are battery-driven, and don't pose much of a threat. However, they are still connected to your amp, so make sure that it is regularly serviced and fitted with a circuit breaker. One problem with pedals is dead batteries, especially with units like digital delays, which will happily eat up a battery in a few hours. The solution is to use "wallwart"-type **AC adapters**, but always buy the correct model from the same manufacturer that made the pedal, as they are all very different! These wall-mounted units deliver the correct current to the pedal via a small socket in the casing, and free you from the worry of deceased Duracells. If you intend to use more than a couple of pedals/adapters then the safest way to deploy them is with a **pedalboard**. Place

your pedals in the their favored order on a piece of plywood and secure them with Velcro pads or elastic loops. Invest in a good **multi-outlet extension box**; this should include a safety **circuit protector** and fuse, and should be large enough to accommodate the adapters side by side. Simply attach this to the pedalboard and connect everything up—not only safe, but a neat way to use your pedals. If you're not handy with a screwdriver, then seek out one of the pre-made pedalboards available from music stores.

Multi-effects often come with AC adapters, but since you are using only one, it is not necessary to make a pedalboard. If you do intend to use extra pedals along with your unit, then a floor-based model, or rack foot controller, can be incorpo-

rated into one large pedalboard. Rack-mounted effects may use a combination of AC cords and adapters; in this case a protected extension box also makes sense. If in doubt, seek advice from the retailer or manufacturer.

A final word on rack-mount systems: Some players use a single rack unit for effects, making a large rack case seem like a pointless investment. However, these cases are sometimes available in smaller sizes and do a great job of protecting your effects. If that still seems unnecessary, then check out some of the inexpensive stands that provide a safe place for your effects to sit, rather than having them wobble precariously over the carrying handle on top of your amp.

Using Effects

Although certain effects are intended to produce specific sounds, this shouldn't stop you from really messing with them. Remember, most effects came about through experimentation and even lucky accidents—a nudged tape spool and an overloaded recording channel brought flanging and distortion to the world! If you have a multi-effects unit, push the parameters to their extremes and try the effects in different combinations; you never know what you might come up with. The same goes for pedals: Try them in different orders with different settings, in and out of the effects loop, everything "on 10." Effects are here to inspire us and produce different sounds, so make sure you try everything they have to offer.

Multi-Effects

When you first try a multi-effects unit, there will probably be a load of factory presets that are intended to show what the product is capable of. Many of these are very usable, offering some good basic sounds; others are all-out, Spielberg-ain't-got-nuthin-on-us patches that may be impressive but are unlikely to be used for anything more than scaring your sister. The important thing is to look at the way these parameters have been set for the sounds that interest you. These can be used as templates for writing your own sounds in the user patches. Start by setting your amp with a good clean sound, with the tone controls set flat, i.e., everything at 5 on the 0-to-10 scale. Adjust the **master volume** on the effects unit so the bypassed signal sounds clear and distortion-free through the amp. Start with a preset you like, then adjust the parameters, using the manual as a guide, until the tone sounds natural and not overly fizzy through the amp. This usually requires reducing some of the high frequencies in the effect's EQ section and using more subtle settings for some effects.

Once you like what you hear you can store it in the memory and move on to the next patch, and repeat until the memory is full. Organize the patches in banks that make it easy to access sounds you intend to use with each other, e.g., one bank per song, containing the sounds you want to use in that song. Finally, do take the time to read the manual. It can be tedious, but it will enlighten you on all of the many functions your effects units are capable of.

Stompboxes

The accepted order for linking pedals together is as follows: compressor, wah-wah, distortion, chorus, delay, then other digital-based effects (harmonizer, flanger, reverb, etc.). This obviously doesn't include every effect, nor does it indicate the position of analog effects, or if a digital flanger should come before or after a digital reverb. The reason? Quite simple; this is just a guideline and different pedals behave very differently depending on their order. Sometimes they sound great, sometimes they sound disgusting, and sometimes they work in ways you never expected. It is impossible to predict how every permutation will sound, and it really boils down to personal taste. Try the above sequence, but try everything else too. It is also worth trying any time-based effects (delay, flanger, chorus, tremolo, etc.) in your amps effects loop. They work more efficiently in that routing, and generally produce more pleasing sounds. If you are intending to build a pedalboard, simply arrange the effects in your preferred sequence and use extra leads to put those effects into the loop. When assembling your pedals, work with one at a time, adjusting the settings to your liking. Also try each pedal in different combinations, making further adjustments, until those you want to use together work together. It really is a case of spending a rainy day on your knees tweaking knobs, but you'll have fun—honest.

Tone Recipes

Instead of letting you leave empty-handed, it only seemed fair to offer some old family recipes for the road. For the sake of simplicity, these are described in the running order **from guitar to amp**, with approximate settings for effects pedals through a clean amplifier with the tone set flat (unless otherwise described).

Multi-effects users should simply select the same effects and adjust the parameters accordingly.

Luscious Thick Clean

- compressor (medium threshold)
- chorus (medium rate, medium depth)
- reverb (medium depth)

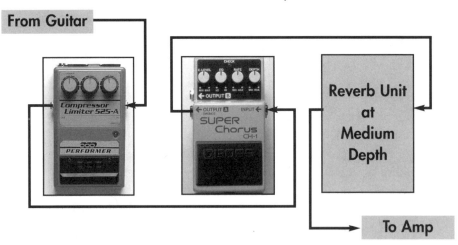

Dead-Dog Blues

- wah-wah (medium)
  - overdrive (low)
    - reverb (high)

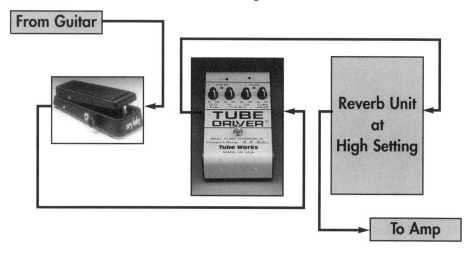

Rockabilly Riffing

- distortion (low)
- delay (high time, medium feedback)
  - reverb (medium/high depth)

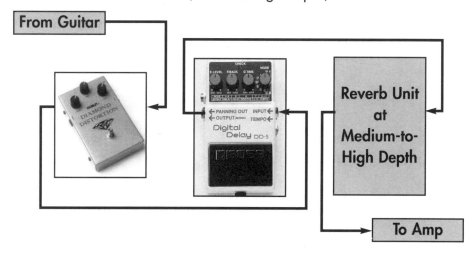

Vintage Van Halen

- distortion (high)
- delay (medium time, low feedback)
- phaser (low rate, medium depth)

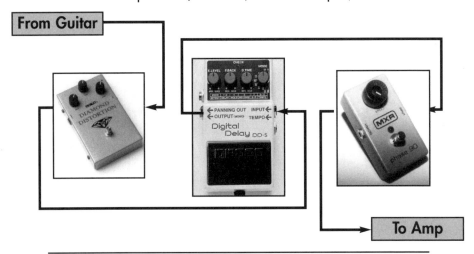

Pink Floyd

- compressor (medium threshold)
- distortion (medium)
- chorus (low rate, low depth)
- delay (low time, medium/high feedback)

Wailing Hendrix
- wah-wah (high)
- fuzz (all the way up!)
- phaser (medium rate, low depth)
- amp (medium/high gain)

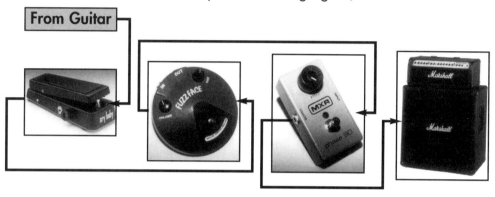

Metallica Monster-Riff
- distortion (high)
- EQ (low frequencies high, medium frequencies low, high frequencies high)*
- reverb (medium)

*This is a scooped sound and can be achieved using the amp's low, medium and treble tone controls.

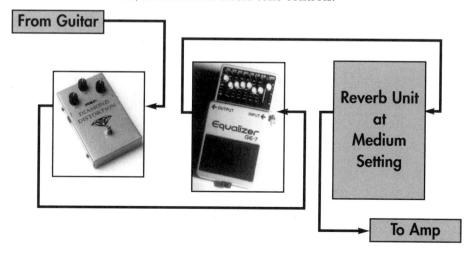

75

Dinosaur Boogie

- distortion (high)
- auto-wah (medium/high threshold)
- octaver (octave below, medium mix)

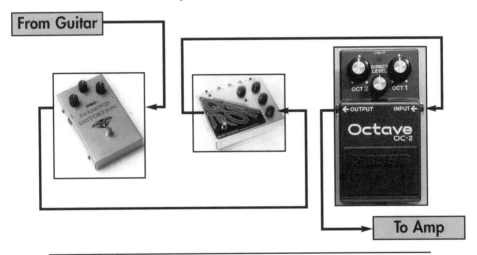

Cheesy Hammond

- distortion (medium)
- octaver (octave below, medium mix)
- chorus (high rate, high depth)
- reverb (medium/high)

Gurgling Zapp-o-rama

- fuzz (high)
- wah-wah (high)
- distortion (medium/high)
- phaser (low rate, high depth)
- tremolo (medium/high rate)
- reverb (high)

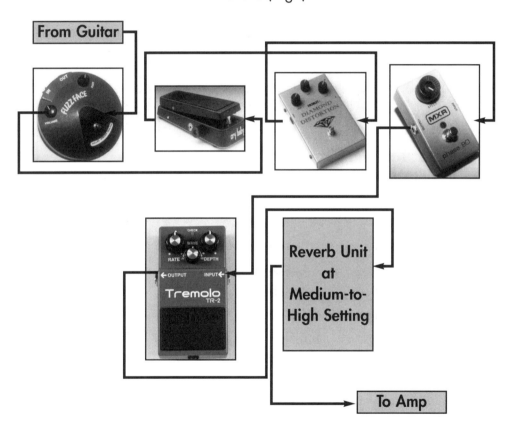

Hope you enjoyed my grandma's recipes. Happy stomping!

Additional Guides from Hal Leonard Corporation

DOD Presents 87 Superstar Guitar Sounds on a Stompbox Budget—Revised

By Eric Mangum and Dean Stubbs

Straight from the pages of Guitar magazine. Learn how you can use affordable FX pedals to duplicate the high-tech sounds of rock's greatest guitarists. Includes guitar setups and recorded samples of such artists as Beck, Clapton, Hammett, Hendrix, Johnson, Malmsteen, Rhoads, Satriani, Van Halen and more!

02503100 ....(104 pages, 9" X 12") $14.95

The Guitar F/X Cookbook

by Chris Amelar

The ultimate source for guitar tricks, effects and other unorthodox techniques! This book demonstrates and explains 45 incredible guitar sounds using common stompboxes and a few unique techniques. Sounds include: pick scraping, police siren, ghost slide, church bell, jaw harp, delay swells, seagull call, gargling, looping, monkey's scream, cat's meow, race car, pickup tapping and many more. Features lots of diagrams and close-up photos of finger positions.

00695080 ....(56 pages, 9" X 12") $14.95

The Stompbox
A History of Guitar Fuzzes, Flangers, Phasers, Echoes & Wahs

by Art Thompson

Stompboxes are fuzz boxes, wah-wah pedals, reverb, tremolo and other add-on devices electric guitarists use to distort and sculpt their instrument's sound, creating outrageous effects. Packed with 200 photos, this entertaining book depicts the development of these odd little analog units, and describes how they're making a comeback—even over today's digital effects.

00330331 ....(160 pages, 7-1/4" X 11") $24.95

Guitar Synth & MIDI

This is the first book to explain the new guitar revolution in both theory and practice. Includes the history and development of guitar synthesizers, basic synthesis, MIDI, sampling, triggering, and explanations of how particular artists like Andy Summers, Al DiMeola, Robert Fripp, Lee Ritenour and others are currently using synthesis and MIDI in their own guitar playing. From choosing equipment to using it, for recording or onstage performance, here is essential information and inspiration for every modern guitarist.

00183704 ....(144 pages, 9" X 12") $14.95

The Recording Guitarist
The Essential Reference Guide for Home & Studio

by Jon Chappell

This is a practical, hands-on guide to a variety of recording environments, from modest home studios where the guitarist must also act as the engineer and producer to professional facilities outfitted with top-quality gear and staffed with audio engineers. This book will prepare guitarists for any recording situation and will help them become familiar with all facets of recording technology and procedure. Topics covered include: guitars and amps for recording; effects; mixer logic and routing strategies; synching music to moving images; and how to look and sound professional, with advice from Alex Lifeson, Carl Verheyen, Steve Lukather, Eric Johnson and others. Also includes complete info on the classic setups of 14 guitar greats from Hendrix to Vai.

00330335 ....(200 pages, 8-1/2" x 11") $19.95

Guitar World Presents: The Bonehead's Guides

The Bonehead's Guide to Guitars

by Dominic Hilton

Don't know your tremolo from your truss rod? Fear not, this book will guide you through the essential differences between various electric guitars, with clear explanations of how they work, how they sound and how their parts function. Learn about the effect that different construction, woods and components have on the tone of a guitar, and how to use this knowledge to get the most from your instrument and track down your ideal electric.

This guide also includes vital information on which guitar to choose for your style of playing and budget, and how to avoid buying a problem instrument. It also contains valuable advice on maintaining and upgrading your guitar, and covers all of the safety precautions associated with using an electrified instrument.
00695332 .... $9.95

The Bonehead's Guide to Amps

by Dominic Hilton

For many novice players their amp is the boring, functional part of their first setup. This guide explains how it can be as exciting, inspirational and important as their guitar. Viewing the amp as an instrument in its own right, this book defines both the fundamental and subtle differences between many types of amplifiers, while offering valuable info on "tone-tweaking" every kind to suit different styles. Learn how to adjust your amp for a whole range of different tones and how to use its functions to maximum effect.

By taking an objective and comprehensive view of available guitar amps, this book offers the best bang-for-buck advice on getting killer tones easily, affordably and blasting at the right level. If you want to get your guitar cooking, then make sure it has the right ingredients with this invaluable guide.
00695334 .... $9.95

The Bonehead's Guide to Effects

by Dominic Hilton

The bizarre technology of guitar effects uses everything from feet to floppy disks, and this guide provides the necessary knowledge to choose and apply these weird devices according to your style and budget. If you feel the urge to wah, flange, uni-vibe or pitch-shift, then this is the book to get you effected.

The Bonehead's Guide to Effects gets right to the point with an illustrated description of every type of guitar effect, including its sound, application and the various formats available. From a simple "stompbox" to high-powered rack systems, all are clearly explained in terms of how they function and how they can be used to enhance your playing.

The text includes a detailed buyer's guide to assembling your ideal effects system, alongside useful safety and maintenance tips. There is also vital info on "chaining" effects and recipes for basic tones and outrageous sounds.
00695333 .... $9.95

FOR MORE INFORMATION, SEE YOUR LOCAL MUSIC DEALER,
OR WRITE TO:

HAL•LEONARD®
CORPORATION
7777 W. BLUEMOUND RD. P.O. BOX 13819 MILWAUKEE, WI 53213

Visit our website at
www.halleonard.com

GUITAR WORLD

PRESENTS

Guitar World Presents is an ongoing series of books filled with extraordinary interviews, feature pieces and instructional material that have made *Guitar World* magazine the world's most popular musicians magazine. For years, *Guitar World* has brought you the most timely, the most accurate and the most hard hitting news and views about your favorite players. Now you can have it all in one convenient package: *Guitar World Presents.*

Guitar World Presents Classic Rock
00330370 (304 pages, 6" x 9") $17.95

Guitar World Presents Alternative Rock
00330369 (352 pages, 6" x 9") $17.95

Guitar World Presents Nirvana and the Grunge Revolution
00330368 (240 pages, 6" x 9") $16.95

Guitar World Presents Kiss
00330291 (144 pages, 6" x 9") $14.95

Guitar World Presents Van Halen
00330294 (208 pages, 6" x 9") $14.95

Guitar World Presents Metallica
00330292 (144 pages, 6" x 9") $14.95

Guitar World Presents Stevie Ray Vaughan
00330293 (144 pages, 6" x 9") $14.95

FOR MORE INFORMATION, SEE YOUR LOCAL MUSIC DEALER, OR WRITE TO:

HAL•LEONARD®
CORPORATION
7777 W. BLUEMOUND RD. P.O. BOX 13819 MILWAUKEE, WI 53213

Prices and availability subject to change without notice.
Some products may not be available outside the U.S.A.